LIFE COACH
SUCCESSFUL WOMEN

MW00718824

THE

ACCOMPLISHED

WOMAN

Success Comes To Those Who Work For It

Sophia Clarkson

Table of Contents

PART 1

Chapter 1:

How Luck Is Created From Success

Success and luck, just two simple words with meaning more profound than the ocean. These words are interrelated. For everyone, success has a different meaning because everyone has a distant dream to fulfill. Some people want a simple life, but some want to live with the luxuries of life. "Dream big" we all have heard this; setting high goals for the future proves that you believe in yourself, that you can do it after it is only you that can make you a success. Some people believe in luck, but luck goes hand in hand with hard work, determination, creativity. To earn the victory, you will always have to work hard, and you can't just leave everything on luck. But how can you make your luck from success? One may ask.

There are a few simple steps to make your luck. When you face a failure, don't just give up yet, don't ever assume that you can't do anything about the situation. It would be best if you decided to take control. It would help if you believed that you could handle the situation and fix the problems; when has giving up ever been suitable for someone's life. When you decide to take control of things, things turn out to be just fine.

As I said before, believing in yourself is a significant part of making your luck. Do something now. Stop postponing things you want to do, gather some willpower, and do it now before it's too late. Another thing you can do to learn to be lucky is to sit back and make a list of various options; if you can't follow up on one of the options, then go for the other one. Think about as many options as you can; just be creative.

When something holds us back, it is tough for us to move forward, or when you are stuck at the same routine and are not doing anything to move forward, luck can do nothing about your laziness. Take out time for yourself and decide about how you will move forward, how you will grow. Consider every single alternative out there. After determining what you want to do in the future, seek the opportunities. Whenever you think you have a chance, take action; now is not the time to sit back and watch; it is the time to run and grab that opportunity because you never know when the next time will come.

Successful people are committed to the fact that they want to be in control of their lives; that is how you make your luck from your success. It's all about believing in yourself.

Chapter 2:

Do More of What Already Works

In 2004, nine hospitals in Michigan began implementing a new procedure in their intensive care units (I.C.U.). Almost overnight, healthcare professionals were stunned by its success.

Three months after it began, the procedure had cut the infection rate of I.C.U. Patients by sixty-six percent. Within 18 months, this one method had saved 75 million dollars in healthcare expenses. Best of all, this single intervention saved the lives of more than 1,500 people in just a year and a half. The strategy was immediately published in a blockbuster paper for the New England Journal of Medicine.

This medical miracle was also simpler than you could ever imagine. It was a checklist.

This five-step checklist was the simple solution that Michigan hospitals used to save 1,500 lives. Think about that for a moment. There were no technical innovations. There were no pharmaceutical discoveries or cutting-edge procedures. The physicians just stopped skipping steps. They implemented the answers they already had on a more consistent basis.

New Solutions vs. Old Solutions

We tend to undervalue answers that we have already discovered. We underutilize old solutions—even best practices—because they seem like something we have already considered.

Here's the problem: *"Everybody already knows that"* is very different from *"Everybody already does that."* Just because a solution is known doesn't mean it is utilized.

Even more critical, just because a solution is implemented occasionally doesn't mean it is implemented consistently. Every physician knew the five steps on Peter Pronovost's checklist, but very few did all five steps flawlessly each time.

We assume that new solutions are needed to make real progress, but that isn't always the case. This pattern is just as present in our personal lives as it is in corporations and governments. We waste the resources and ideas at our fingertips because they don't seem new and exciting.

There are many examples of behaviors, big and small, that have the opportunity to drive progress in our lives if we just did them with more consistency—flossing every day—never missing workouts. Performing fundamental business tasks each day, not just when you have time—apologizing more often. Writing Thank You notes each week.

Of course, these answers are boring. Mastering the fundamentals isn't sexy, but it works. No matter what task you are working on, a simple checklist of steps you can follow right now—fundamentals that you have known about for years—can immediately yield results if you just practice them more consistently.

Progress often hides behind boring solutions and underused insights. You don't need more information. You don't need a better strategy. You just need to do more of what already works.

Chapter 3:

Figuring Out Your Dreams

Today we're going to talk about dreams and why it is important that we all have some form of a dream or aspiration that we can work towards.

For many of us who are educated in the traditional school system, we process from one grade to the next without much thought and planning besides getting into a good school. And this autopilot has caused many kids, including myself, to not have a vision of my future and what I would like to become when I grow up. We are all taught in some shape or form that we would need to choose a career and pursue that path. Dedicating years of higher education and hundreds of hours of curriculum work only to find ourselves hating the course that we had spent all this time and energy undertaking when we step into our jobs.

This has caused many to start doubting and questioning what we ought to really do with our lives and we might get really anxious because this was certainly not part of the plan that we had set out since we were young.

What I have found personally is that I spent the time and effort to pursue a higher education not because I really wanted To, but rather to appease my parents that they did not waste all their time and money on producing me with proper schooling.

I did not however, go into my field of practice that I had spent the prior 3 years studying for. Instead upon graduating, that was when I really started to figure out what I really wanted to do with my life. Luckily for my parents, they were willing to give me the time and space to explore different possible passions and to carve out a path on my own.

I realised that as I started exploring more, and learning more about myself, the dream that I thought i once had started to change. Instead of dreaming of the perfect job and having the perfect boss, I now dreamt of freedom. To achieve freedom of time to pursue my passions, and to take steps that would move me one step closer to that dream as soon as possible.

Why this particular dream you ask? As i started exploring on successful people who have made it big in life, I realized that those that were truly happy with what they were doing, were not doing things for the money, but rather that they were able to quit their full time jobs to pursue their interests because somehow they had found a way to achieve time freedom that is irrespective of money. It amazed me how many found success by having the freedom to work from home, to not be bound by a desk job or to be hounded on my their bosses. Some live for the climb up the corporate ladder, but i knew that wasn't going to work for me. And I knew i had to make something else work to survive.

So i decided to dedicate my time and energy to only doing things that would help me achieve freedom and that became my dream to retire early and live off my past works.

The takeaway for today is that I want you to give yourself the chance to explore different things and take a step back to assess whether your current dream will actually serve you well in the long run, or if u don't even have a dream, whether you need to take time off to go find that dream for yourself.

I challenge each and everyone of you today to keep an open mind that dreams can change and you can always pursue a new path should you choose to. Because as the saying goes, the only constant in life is change.

Take care and I'll see you in the next one.

5 Tips for A More Creative Brain

Nearly all great ideas follow a similar creative process, and this article explains how this process works. Understanding this is important because creative thinking is one of the most useful skills you can possess. Nearly every problem you face in work and life can benefit from creative solutions, lateral thinking, and innovative ideas.

Anyone can learn to be creative by using these five steps. That's not to say being creative is easy. Uncovering your creative genius requires courage and tons of practice. However, this five-step approach should help demystify the creative process and illuminate the path to more innovative thinking.

To explain how this process works, let me tell you a short story.

A Problem in Need of a Creative Solution

In the 1870s, newspapers, and printers faced a very specific and very costly problem. Photography was a new and exciting medium at the time. Readers wanted to see more pictures, but nobody could figure out how to print images quickly and cheaply.

For example, if a newspaper wanted to print an image in the 1870s, they had to commission an engraver to etch a copy of the photograph onto a steel plate by hand. These plates were used to press the image onto the page, but they often broke after a few uses. This process of photoengraving, you can imagine, was remarkably time-consuming and expensive.

The man who invented a solution to this problem was named Frederic Eugene Ives. He became a trailblazer in the field of photography and held over 70 patents by the end of his career. His story of creativity and innovation, which I will share now, is a useful case study for understanding the five key steps of the creative process.

A Flash of Insight

Ives got his start as a printer's apprentice in Ithaca, New York. After two years of learning the ins and outs of the printing process, he began managing the photographic laboratory at nearby Cornell University. He spent the rest of the decade experimenting with new photography techniques and learning about cameras, printers, and optics.

In 1881, Ives had a flash of insight regarding a better printing technique.

"While operating my photo stereotypes process in Ithaca, I studied the problem of the halftone process," Ives said. "I went to bed one night in a state of brain fog over the problem, and the instant I woke in the morning saw before me, apparently projected on the ceiling, the completely worked out process and equipment in operation."

Ives quickly translated his vision into reality and patented his printing approach in 1881. He spent the remainder of the decade improving upon it. By 1885, he had developed a simplified process that delivered even better results. As it came to be known, the Ives Process reduced the cost of printing images by 15x and remained the standard printing technique for the next 80 years.

Alright, now let's discuss what lessons we can learn from Ives about the creative process.

The 5 Stages of the Creative Process

In 1940, an advertising executive named James Webb Young published a short guide titled, A Technique for Producing Ideas. In this guide, he made a simple but profound statement about generating creative ideas.

According to Young, innovative ideas happen when you develop new combinations of old elements. In other words, creative thinking is not about generating something new from a blank slate but rather about taking what is already present and combining those bits and pieces in a way that has not been done previously.

Most importantly, generating new combinations hinges upon your ability to see the relationships between concepts. If you can form a new link between two old ideas, you have done something creative.

Young believed this process of creative connection always occurred in five steps.

1. **Gather new material.** At first, you learn. During this stage, you focus on 1) learning specific material directly related to your task and 2) learning general material by becoming fascinated with a wide range of concepts.

2. **Thoroughly work over the materials in your mind.** During this stage, you examine what you have learned by looking at the facts from different angles and experimenting with fitting various ideas together.

3. **Step away from the problem.** Next, you put the problem completely out of your mind and do something else that excites you and energizes you.

4. **Let your idea return to you.** At some point, but only after you stop thinking about it will your idea come back to you with a flash of insight and renewed energy.

5. **Shape and develop your idea based on feedback.** For any idea to succeed, you must release it out into the world, submit it to criticism, and adapt it as needed.

Chapter 4:

8 Ways To Deal With Setbacks In Life

Life is never the same for anyone - It is an ever-changing phenomenon, making you go through all sorts of highs and lows. And as good times are an intrinsic part of your life, so are bad times. One day you might find yourself indebted by 3-digit figures while having only $40 in your savings account. Next day, you might be vacationing in Hawaii because you got a job that you like and pays $100,000 a year. There's absolutely no certainty to life (except passing away) and that's the beauty of it. You never know what is in store for you. But you have to keep living to see it for yourself. Setbacks in life cannot be avoided by anyone. Life will give you hardships, troubles, break ups, diabetes, unpaid bills, stuck toilet and so much more. It's all a part of your life.

Here's 8 ways that you might want to take notes of, for whenever you may find yourself in a difficult position in dealing with setback in life.

1. Accept and if possible, embrace it

The difference between accepting and embracing is that when you accept something, you only believe it to be, whether you agree or disagree. But when you embrace something, you truly KNOW it to be true and accept it as a whole. There is no dilemma or disagreement after you have embraced something.

So, when you find yourself in a difficult situation in life, accept it for what it is and make yourself whole-heartedly believe that this problem in your life, at this specific time, is a part of your life. This problem is what makes you complete. This problem is meant for you and only you can go through it. And you will. Period. There can be no other way.

The sooner you embrace your problem, the sooner you can fix it. Trying to bypass it will only add upon your headaches.

2. Learn from it

Seriously, I can't emphasize how important it is to LEARN from the setbacks you face in your life. Every hardship is a learning opportunity. The more you face challenges, the more you grow. Your capabilities expand with every issue you solve—every difficulty you go through, you rediscover yourself. And when you finally deal off with it, you are reborn. You are a new person with more wisdom and experience.

When you fail at something, try to explore why you failed. Be open-minded about scrutinizing yourself. Why couldn't you overcome a certain situation? Why do you think of this scenario as a 'setback'? The moment you find the answers to these questions is the moment you will have found the solution.

3. Execute What You Have Learnt

The only next step from here is to execute that solution and make sure that the next time you face a similar situation, you'll deal with it by having both your arms tied back and blindfolded. All you have to do is remember what you did in a similar past experience and reapply your previous solution.

Thomas A. Edison, the inventor of the light bulb, failed 10,000 times before finally making it. And he said "I have not failed. I just found 10,000 ways that won't work".

The lesson here is that you have to take every setback as a lesson, that's it.

4. Without shadow, you can never appreciate light

This metaphor is applicable to all things opposite in this universe. Everything has a reciprocal; without one, the other cannot exist. Just as without shadow, we wouldn't have known what light is, similarly, without light, we could've never known about shadow. The two opposites identify and complete each other.

Too much of philosophy class, but to sum it up, your problems in life, ironically, is exactly why you can enjoy your life. For example, if you are a chess player, then defeating other chess players will give you enjoyment while getting defeated will give you distress. But, when you are a chess prodigy—you have defeated every single chess player on earth and there's no one else to defeat, then what will you do to derive pleasure? Truth is, you can now no longer enjoy chess. You have no one to defeat. No one gives you the fear of losing anymore and as a result, the taste of winning has lost its appeal to you.

So, whenever you face a problem in life, appreciate it because without it, you can't enjoy the state of not having a problem. Problems give you the pleasure of learning from them and solving them.

5. View Every Obstacle As an opportunity

This one's especially for long term hindrances to your regular life. The COVID-19 pandemic for instance, has set us back for almost two years now. As distressing it is, there is also some positive impact of it. A long-term setback opens up a plethora of new avenues for you to explore. You suddenly get a large amount of time to experiment with things that you have never tried before.

When you have to pause a regular part of your life, you can do other things in the meantime. I believe that every one of us has a specific talent and most people never know what their talent is simply because they have never tried that thing.

6. Don't Be Afraid to experiment

People pursue their whole life for a job that they don't like and most of them never ever get good at it. As a result, their true talent gets buried under their own efforts. Life just carries on with unfound potential. But when some obstacle comes up and frees you from the clutches of doing what you have been doing for a long time, then you should get around and experiment. Who knows? You, a bored high school teacher, might be a natural at tennis. You won't know it unless you are fired from that job and actually play tennis to get over it. So whenever life gives you lemons, quit trying to hold on to it. Move on and try new things instead.

7. Stop Comparing yourself to others

The thing is, we humans are emotional beings. We become emotionally vulnerable when we are going through something that isn't supposed to be. And in such times, when we see other people doing fantastic things in life, it naturally makes us succumb to more self-loathing. We think lowly of our own selves and it is perfectly normal to feel this way. Talking and comapring ourselves to people who are seemingly untouched by setbacks is a counterproductive move. You will listen to their success-stories and get depressed—lose self-esteem. Even if they try their best to advise you, it won't get through to you. You won't be able to relate to them.

8. Talk to people other people who are having their own setbacks in life

I'm not asking you to talk to just any people. I'm being very specific here: talk to people who are going through bad times as well.

If you start talking to others who are struggling in life, perhaps more so compared to you, then you'll see that everyone else is also having difficulties in life. It will seem natural to you. Moreover, having talked with others might even show you that you are actually doing better than all these other people. You can always find someone who is dealing with more trouble than you and that will enlighten you. That will encourage you. If someone else can deal with tougher setbacks in life, why can't you?

Besides, listening to other people will give you a completely new perspective that you can use for yourself if you ever find yourself in a similar situation as others whom you have talked with.

Conclusion

Setbacks are a part of life. Without them we wouldn't know what the good times are. Without them we wouldn't appreciate the success that we have gotten. Without them we wouldn't cherish the moments that got us to where we are heading to. And without them there wouldn't be any challenge to fill our souls with passion and fire. Take setbacks as a natural process in the journey. Use it to fuel your drive. Use it to move your life forward one step at a time.

Chapter 5:

12 Things to Do When You Feel Overwhelmed

Sometimes we get overwhelmed and are completely clueless as to what we should do the trick with that it is to reset quickly so you can recover and get back to what you need to do and things you have to do. Here are 12 of the best tactics to make that happen.

1. Take An Emotional Time Out

Try reading an engaging book that is not related to the work you are currently doing or go and watch a nice movie. The goal here is to take an hour and two away from your problems- physically someplace else if that is possible. This will help you remember that there is a vast world out there and will put you back in perspective.

2. Take A Physical Time Out

Make yourself move a bit; you can hit the gym or go for a run or swim, take a dance class, whatever it is you do for exercise, try to work it in the middle of the day; that way, you will be able to separate your difficult morning from the rest of your day. Once more, you can emotionally separate yourself from your worries.

3. Breathe Deeply

This is a shorter and much more effective and practical way. All you need to do is take a full 120 seconds to breathe in and out very deeply, maybe go for 6 or 7 breaths per minute, and by the end, you will feel a bit better than before.

4. Be Mindfully Thankful

If you are here right now reading this, you should be thankful you are alive at one of the greatest times, using a device that lets you connect with the entire history of the world's knowledge basically for free and with just one click. Hopefully, you have people in your life that love you. Even if you do not realize it right away, you still have people like that in your life. You know what? Things are pretty good, no matter how rough they might seem at any particular moment. Take a minute, reflect, and reset.

5. Pray Or Meditate

Whatever is your way of connecting with the higher power, you should spend a few minutes daily doing it. This will be important for you in the process of grounding, and you will stay connected to your surroundings.

6. Phone A Friend

Sometimes all you need is a chance to talk with someone you're close with who is completely unrelated to whatever momentary drama is going on in your life. Catching up with old buddies can be refreshing. It can remind you of all the good time you have spent and gives you a break from whatever is currently going on in your life.

7. Delegate

Do you have to do it all yourself? If the answer is no, then don't. Share the load. And don't forget, you don't have to be the boss to delegate. You can often simply ask colleagues and friends for help. They'll give you the chance to return the favor sometime.

8. Write Stuff Down

Sometimes things become more manageable when you write them down. A top military officer I knew kept a journal during the invasion of Iraq. He was so worried and stressed that he only had time to write one haiku per day, but it helped him keep his head on straight.

9. Take A Nap

Everything looks a bit better in the morning and also after you have taken a 30-min catnap. This might not be the most practical suggestion if you work for someone else, but if you're your own boss, then it's perfect you can do things on your own terms, which means you can sneak a nap in between work.

10. Map Your Progress

Create a to-do list in which you can include things you have already done. All you have to do is go back and cross those things out. You will be able to put in perspective how much you have achieved in a day, especially on a particularly rough day.

11. Drink (Water)

Studies have shown increasing your water intake improves your mood. Even though it's supposed to take longer than just drinking a bottle or two, I find that water has a placebo effect. It makes you feel better because you know you're doing something small that's health-positive.

12. Turn Stuff Down

Sometimes you just need to say no. Sometimes you even have to say, "I know I said yes before--but I have to say no now." Of course, you don't want to do a practice this and develop a reputation for unreliability. Still, maybe it's better than getting overwhelmed and getting nothing done.

Chapter 6:

8 Ways To Adopt New ThoughtsThat Will Be Beneficial To Your Life

"Each morning we are born again. What we do today is what matters most." - Buddha

Is your glass half-empty or half-full? Answering this age-old question may reflect your outlook on life, your attitude toward yourself, whether you're optimistic or pessimistic, or it may even affect your health. Studies show that personality traits such as optimism and pessimism play a considerable role in determining your health and well-being. The positive thinking that comes with optimism is a practical part of stress management. Positive thinking in no way means that we keep our heads in the sand and ignore life's less pleasant situations. Instead, you have to approach the unpleasantness more positively and productively. Always think that something best is going to happen, and ignore the worst-case scenarios.

Here are some ways for you to adopt new thoughts that will benefit your outlook on life.

1. Breaking Out Old Thinking Patterns

We all can get stuck in a loop of specific thoughts. Sure, they may look comfortable on the outside, but we don't realize that these thoughts are what's holding us back most of the time. It's crucial to let fresh ideas and thoughts into your life and break away from the negative ones to see new paths ahead. We could start by challenging our assumptions in every situation. We may already assume what's about to happen if we fall into some condition, but trying new preconceptions can open up some exciting possibilities for us.

2. Rephrase The Problem

Your creativity can get limited by how you define or frame your problems. If you keep on looking at the problem from one side only, chances are you won't get much exposure to the solution. Whereas, if you look at it in different ways and different angles, new solutions can emerge. For example, the founder of Uber, Garret Camp, could have focused on buying and managing enough vehicles for him to make a profit. Instead, he looked more into how he could best entertain the passengers and thus, made a powerful app for their comfort.

3. Think In Reverse

Try turning the problem upside-down if you're having difficulties finding a new approach. Flip the situation and explore the opposite of what you want to achieve. This can help you present innovative ways to tackle the real issue. If you're going to take a good picture, try all of its angles first so you can understand which grade will be more suitable and which angles you should avoid. If you want to develop a new design for your website, try its worst look first and then make it the exact opposite. Apply different types of creativity to tackle your problems.

4. Make New Connections

Another way to generate new ideas and beneficial thoughts is by making unique and unexpected connections. Some of the best ideas click to you by chance, you hear or see something utterly unconnected to the situation you're trying to solve, and an idea has occurred to you almost instantly. For instance, architect Mick Pearce developed a groundbreaking climate-control system by taking the concept from the self-cooling mounds built by termites. You can pick on any set of random words, picture prompts, and objects of interest and then look for the novel association between them and your problem.

5. Finding Fresh Perspectives

Adding extra dynamism to your thinking by taking a step back from your usual standpoint and viewing a problem through "fresh eyes" might be beneficial for you to tackle an issue and give new thoughts. You could also talk to someone with a different perspective, life experience, or cultural background and would be surprised to see their approach. Consider yourself being the other person and see life from their eyes, their point of view.

6. Focus On The Good Things

Challenges and struggles are a part of life. When you're faced with obstacles, try and focus on the good part, no matter how seemingly insignificant or small it seems. If you keep looking for it, you will definitely find the proverbial silver lining in every cloud if it's not evident in the beginning.

7. Practice Gratitude

Practicing gratitude is said to reduce stress, foster resilience, and improve self-esteem. If you're going through a bad time, think of people, moments, or things that bring you some kind of comfort and happiness and express your gratitude once in a while. This could be anything, from thanking your loved one to lending a helping hand to anyone.

8. Practice Positive Self-Talk

We sometimes are our own worst critics and tend to be the hardest on ourselves. This can cause you to form a negative opinion of yourself. This could be prevented by practicing positive self-talk. As a result, this could influence your ability to regulate your feelings, thoughts, and behaviors under stress.

Conclusion

Developing a positive attitude can help you in many ways than you might realize. When you practice positive thinking, you consciously or subconsciously don't allow your mind to entertain any negative thoughts. You will start noticing remarkable changes all around you. By reducing your self-limiting beliefs, you will effectively grow as you have never imagined before. You can change your entire outlook on life by harnessing the power of positive thinking. You will also notice a significant boost in your confidence.

Chapter 7:

Knowing When It's Time To Switch Off

Today I'm going to talk about relaxation and off-work time. I hope that by the end of this discussion that I can get you to calm down and just enjoy life a little bit more. Life isn't all about work and no play. We must learn to set boundaries and learn when it is time to work and when it is time to swift off.

For many of us who are workaholics, or those with immensely busy schedules and deadlines, we may find it hard to chill. Having all these problems in the back of our minds, our day becomes consumed with work that we may find it incredibly difficult to disconnect from. We may end up growing distant and not being present with our families when they require our attention. This can affect our relationships negatively in a multitude of ways.

For those of you who have children, not knowing when to switch off and give your full attention to their upbringing can have direct consequences to their growth and development. Furthermore, your children may view you as distant and disengaged. Not being able to get that parental support from you, they may not view you as a pillar of support. Over time your children may learn not to look for you when they need help because you are always either busy with work or too preoccupied to engage with them.

The same goes for your partner. If they don't get the full attention from you during dinner conversations, or that you are constantly replying emails on your phone and messaging your colleagues at all hours of the evening, they might also grow distant to you over time. You see relationships are built on quality time spent together. Whether it be with friends, family, partners, or kids. They all operate on the same principle.

Which is why knowing when to switch off and give your relationships the quality time it needs is very important.

Not knowing when to switch off also has other consequences. It robs us of joy. It robs us of our free time because we don't set boundaries between work and play. We give our colleagues 24 hour assess to us, knowing that we will be available all hours of the day no matter the time. This frequent intrusion into our personal time is unfortunately the culture that some companies choose to adopt. Depending on how you feel about it and your circumstance, it is my opinion that this isn't the best work culture to be in if it happens all year round.

When your employers expect you to work past your work hours every single day, you might want to think twice about whether this sacrifice is worth your time and money. Whether the trade off is worth putting your relationships and obligations on the line. Whether your time is worth more or less than the company is paying to take away from you. Only you can make that decision for yourself.

Another problem that all of us face with the pandemic is that many of us are forced to work from home. While this can sound like a good thing for many of us, in some ways it can make it difficult to draw the line between work and rest. Having the freedom to work all hours of the day makes it harder for us to stay focused on the job, and many times we can't separate the parts of the day that is meant for work and the parts that are meant for rest. Studies have shown that we spend more time working when we are at home because we simply don't know when it is time to stop and switch off.

This phenomenon actually resonates with me as I too work from home. And my work day tends to stretch from the minute I wake up, to the last hour before I hit the hay. Setting clear boundaries becomes much more difficult and requires a great deal of discipline.

To sum it all up, knowing when to switch off actually requires an active commitment on our part to set the boundaries we need and to stick to it religiously. We should define the time of day in our week that are meant for work and the times that are meant for family and friends. And that means no work calls, no emails, no checking on company group messages, and no work laptops during those times.

By following these rules strictly, we can then give ourselves the time and space we need to recharge, rest, spend time with family, and then come back to work ready for another day.

I hope you have learned something today. Take care and I'll see you in the next one.

Chapter 8:

NOTHING IS IMPOSSIBLE

Success is a concept as individual as beauty is, in the eye of the beholder, but with each individuals success comes testing circumstances, the price that must be paid in advance.

The grind,

The pain and the losses all champions have endured.

These hardships are no reason to quit but an indicator that you are heading in the right direction, because we must walk through the rain to see the rainbow and we must endure loss to make space for our new desired results.

Often the bigger the desired change , the bigger the pain, and this is why so few do it.

The very fact that are listening to this right now says to me you have something extra about you.

Inside you know there is more for you and that dream you have, you believe it is possible.

If others have done it before, then so can you , because we can do anything we set our minds and hearts to.

But we must take control of our destiny, have clear results in mind and take calculated action towards those results.

The path may be foggy and unknown but as you commit to the result and believe in it the path, it will be revealed soon enough.

We don't need to know the how, to declare we are going to do something, the how will come later.

Clear commitment to the result is key .

Too many people never live their dreams because they don't know how.

The how can be found out always if we can commit and believe fully in the process.

Faith is the magic elixir to success, without it nothing is possible.

What you believe about you is everything

If you believe you cannot swim and your dream is to be an Olympic swimming champion, what are your chances?

Any rational person would say, well learn to swim,

How many of you want to be multi-millionaires?

I guess everyone?

How many out there know how to get to such a status?

Would we just give up and say it is impossible?

Or would it be as logical as simply learning how to swim or ride a bike?

We believe someone could be an Olympic swimming champion with training and practice , but not a multi-millionaire?

Many of us think big goals are simply too unrealistic.

Fear of failure , fear of what people might think , fear of change , all common reasons for aiming low in life.

But when we aim low and succeed the disappointment in that success is a foul tasting medicine.

Start gaining clarity in the reality of our results.

By thinking bigger we all have the ability to hit what seem now like unrealistic heights, but later realise that nothing is impossible.

We should all start from the assumption that we can do anything, it might take years of training but we can do it. Anything we set our minds to, we can do it.

So ask yourself right now those very important questions.

What exactly would I be doing right now that will make me the happiest person in the world? How much money do I want ?

What kind of relationships do I want?

When You have defined those things clearly,

Set the bar high and accept nothing less.

Because life will pay you any price.

But the time is ticking, you can't have it twice.

Chapter 9:

The Trick To Focusing

If you've been struggling with procrastinations and distractions, just not being able to do the things you know you should do and purposefully putting them off by mindlessly browsing social media or the web, then today I'm going to share with you one very simple trick that has worked for me in getting myself to focus.

I will not beat around the bush for this. The trick is to sit in silence for a minute with your work laid out in front of you in a quiet place free from noise or distractions. I know it sounds silly, but it has worked time and time again for me whenever I did this and I believe it will work the same for you.

You see our brains are constantly racing with a million thoughts. Thoughts telling us whether we should be doing our work, thoughts telling us that we should turn on the TV instead, thoughts that don't serve any real purpose but to pull us away from our goal of doing the things that matter.

Instead of being a victim of our minds, and going according to its whims and fancies. Quieting down the mind by sitting in complete silence is a good way to engage ourselves in a deeper way. A way that cuts the mind off completely, to plug ourselves out of the automated thoughts that don't serve us, and to realign ourselves with our goals and purpose of working.

To do this effectively, it is best that you turn on the AC to a comfortable temperature, sit on your working chair, lay your work out neatly in front of you, and just sit in silence for a moment. What I found that works a step up is to actually put on my noise cancelling headphones, and I find myself disappear into a clear mind. A mind free from noise, distractions, social media, music, and all the possible ways that it can throw me off my focus.

With no noise whatsoever, you will find yourself at complete peace with the world. Your thoughts about procrastination will get crushed by your feelings of serenity and peace. A feeling that you can do anything if you wanted to right now.

Everytime I turned on music or the TV, thinking I needed it as a distraction, my focus always ends up split. I operate on a much lower level of productivity because my mind is in two places. One listening to the TV or music, and the other on my work. I end up wasting more resources of my brain and end up feeling more tired and fatigued quickly than I normally would.

If that sounds familiar to you, well i have been there and done that too. And I can tell you that it is not a sustainable way to go about doing things in the long run.

The power of silence is immense. It keeps us laser focused on the task in front of us. And we hesitate less on every decision.

The next thing I would need you to do is to actually challenge yourself to be distraction free for as long as possible when you first start engaging in silence. Put all your devices on silent mode, keep it vibration free, and do not let notifications suck you back into the world of distractions. It is the number 1 killer of productivity and focus for all of us.

So if u struggle with focusing, I want you to give it a try right. If you know you are distracted there is no harm right here right now to make a choice to give this a shot.

Take out our noise cancelling earphones, turn the ac on, turn your devices off or to silent, lay your work out in front of you, turn up the lights, sit on your chair, close your eyes for a minute, and watch the magic happen.

Chapter 10:

How to Learn Faster

Remember the saying, "You are never too old to learn something new"? Believe me, it's not true in any way you understood it.

The most reliable time to learn something new was the time when you were growing up. That was the time when your brain was in its most hyperactive state and could absorb anything you had thrown at it.

You can still learn, but you would have to change your approach to learning.

You won't learn everything, because you don't like everything going on around you. You naturally have an ego to please. So what can you do to boost your learning? Let's simplify the process. When you decide to learn something, take a moment and ask yourself this; "Will this thing make my life better? Will this fulfill my dreams? Will I benefit from it?".

If you can answer all these questions in a positive, you will pounce on the thing and you won't find anyone more motivated than you.

Learning is your brain's capability to process things constructively. If you pick up a career, you won't find it hard to flourish if you are genuinely interested in that particular skill.

Whether it be sports, singing, entrepreneurship, cooking, writing, or anything you want to pursue. Just ask yourself, can you use it to increase your creativity, your passion, your satisfaction. If you can, you will start learning it as if you knew it all along.

Your next step to learning faster would be to improve and excel at what you already have. How can you do that? It's simple yet again!

Ask yourself another question, that; "Why must I do this? Why do I need this?" if you get to answer that, you will find the fastest and effective way to the top yourself without any coaching. Why will this happen on its own? Because now you have found a purpose for your craft and the destination is clear as the bright sun in the sky.

The last but the most important thing to have a head start on your journey of learning is the simplest of them all, but the hardest to opt for. The most important step is to start working towards things.

The flow of learning is from Head to Heart to Hands. You have thought of the things you want to do in your brain. Then you asked your heart if it satisfied you. Now it's time to put your hands to work.

You never learn until you get the chance to experience the world yourself. When you go through a certain event, your brain starts to process the outcomes that could have been, and your heart tells you to give it one more try. Here is the deciding moment. If you listen to your heart right away, you will get on a path of learning that you have never seen before.

What remains now is your will to do what you have decided. And when you get going, you will find the most useful resources immediately. Use your instincts and capitalize your time. Capture every chance with sheer will and belief as if this is your final moment for your dreams to come true.

It doesn't matter if you are not the ace in the pack, it doesn't matter if you are not in your peak physical shape, it doesn't matter if you don't have the money yet. You will someday get all those things only if you had the right skills and the right moment.

For all you know, this moment right now is the most worth it moment. So don't go fishing in other tanks when you have your own aquarium. That aquarium is your body, mind, and soul. All you need is to dive deep with sheer determination and the stars are your limit.

PART 2

Chapter 1:

Start Working On Your Dreams Today

When did you get up today? What was your day like? What did you achieve today? Did any of that matter?

Maybe it didn't because you don't have any dreams to work towards, or maybe that you've forgotten what they are altogether.

To have a dream is to have a direction in life. To have a dream means you have something bigger than yourself that you want to achieve.

Everyone gets at least one chance in their life to actually go and pursue that dream, but few recognize that until it is too late. It is too late to regret when you are on your deathbed wondering what could have been. That is when it is too late to work on your dreams. When you have no more time left.

The Moment to start working On your dreams is right here right now.

We repeat our failures every day but never learn. We get depressed every day but never communicate. We get bullied every day, but never fight back. Why?

Is it because we can't do it? No, Definitely Not! We can do it whenever we want. We can do it today. We can do it the next minute. We just lack Ambition!

Every day someone achieves something big. Some more than often, others maybe not their whole life. But the outcome is **not** determined by **fate**, but with **Effort**.

All the billionaires you see today started out with a few dollars just like you and me. They just had the guts to pursue their dream no matter what the cost is. They all had a vision of something bigger. They went full throttle even when everyone around them expected them to fail. Even when they met with struggles that hit them harder than the last, they were still focused on the dream. Never did they once lesson the effort.

No two persons are born the same. Not the same face, color, intelligence, or fate. But what's common for every human being is the built-in trait to strive for a goal once they are determined enough. Doesn't matter if it's food for the next meal or success for the times to come.

The struggle is real, it always was, it always will be. The world wouldn't be what it is today if it weren't for the struggle man has gone through over the centuries. The struggle is the most real definition of life in this world. But that doesn't mean it's a bad one.

Our parents struggled to make us a better person. They put in their best effort to watch us succeed in our dreams. Their parents did the same for them and their parents before them.

This is what makes life a cycle of inherited struggle and hardships. Nobody asks to struggle through a hard life, but we can all turn the hard life into a meaningful one. The life that we all should expect to eventually achieve only if we keep the cycle running and if we keep putting in the effort.

How then do we actually work towards our dreams? By focusing on the things that matter each and every day, again and again, until that mountain has been conquered. Don't forget to enjoy the journey, because it could well be the best part of the trip up top.

You never know what the next moment has in it for you. You can never predict the future, but you can always hope for a better one. You only get the right to hope if you did what was meant to be done today. It's your lawful right to reap the fruit if you took care of sowing the seeds faithfully and diligently all through the year.

The motivation behind this continuous grind of time in search of that Dream lies in your past. You cannot achieve those dreams until you start treasuring the lessons of your past and become a person who is always willing to go beyond.

You can't simply depend on hope to get something done. You have to reach the point where start obsessing over that goal, that thing, that DREAM. When you start obsessing, you start working, you start seeing the possibilities and you just keep going. If you don't get up then you WILL miss the moment. The moment that could have made all the difference in the world. If you don't act upon that impulse, you might never get that inspiration ever again. And that will be the moment you will always regret for the rest of your life.

Remember that your whole life is built on millions of tiny decisions. A decision to just act on one of those moments can transform your life completely. These moments often test you too. But only for an inch more before you find eternal glory. So don't wait for someone else to do it for you. Get up, buckle up, and start doing. Because only you Can!

6 Ways To Adopt New Actions That Will Be Beneficial To Your Life

There is this myth that goes around saying that, once you leave your teenage, you can never change your Habits. One can analyze this for themselves. Everyone has a list of new year's resolutions and goals. We hope to get these things done to some extent, but, never do we ever really have a clear idea of how to get to those goals in the least possible time.

We always desire a better future but never really know how to bring the necessary change in our lives. The change we need is a change in attitude and behavior towards life altogether. Change is never easy, but it is achievable with some sheer willpower. You might be on the right track to lead a better life, but there are always more and better things to add to your daily habits that can be helpful in your daily life.

Here are 6 simple yet achievable actions you need to take:

1. Decide Today What Is Most Important In Your Life

Life is a constant search for motivation. The motivation to keep doing and changing for the better. Once you have something to change for, take a moment and envision the rest of your life with and without the change you are about to make.

If you have made up your mind, now think about how you can start off with these things. For starters, if you want a healthy lifestyle, start your day with a healthy breakfast and morning exercise on an empty stomach.

If you want to scale your business, make a customer-friendly business model.

2. Make Reasonable and Achievable Goals.

Adopting new habits can be challenging, especially if you have to change something in your day-to-day life to get better results. Start easy by making goals that are small, easy, reasonable, and won't give you a headache.

You can start off with baby steps. If you want to become more responsible, mature, and sorted in your life, just start your day by making your own bed, and do your dishes. Ride a bicycle to work, instead of a car or a bus. Things become smooth and easier once you have a reason for the hard acts.

3. Erase Distractions from Your Daily Life

You have wasted a lot already, don't waste any more time. As young as you are right now, you should feel more privileged than the older people around you. You have got the luxury of time over them. You have the right energy and pinnacle moments to seize every opportunity you can grasp.

Don't make your life a cluster of meaningless and profit-less distractions. You don't have to go to every public gathering that you are invited to. Only those that give you something in return. Something that you can avail yourself of in your years to come. Don't divulge in these distractions only for the sake of memories. Memories fade but the time you waste will always have its imprint in every moment that follows.

4. Make a Diary and a Music Playlist

You can devote some time to yourself, just to communicate with your brain and start a discussion with yourself. Most people keep a diary for this purpose, some people tend to make a digital one these days. When you start writing to yourself in the third person, talking and discussing your issues and your weaknesses, you tend to find the solutions within.

Most people find it comforting and calming when they have a playlist of music playing in the background while working. Everyone can try this to check if they get a better level of creativity if they have some small activity that soothes their stressed nerves.

5. Incorporate Regular Walk and Exercise in Your Life

When you know you have a whole day ahead of you, where you have to sit in an office chair for the next 8 hours. Where you have to sit in your home office looking at those sheets for most of the day. A 10 min walk before or after the busy schedule can help a lot in such conditions. You can never avoid physical activities for your whole life, especially if you want to live a healthier and longer life.

People always feel reluctant to exercise and running once they enter college or work life. Especially once they have a family to look out for. But trust me, your body needs that blood rushing once a day for some time. You will feel much more pumped and motivated after a hard 2-mile jog or a 15 min workout.

6. Ask Others for Help and Advice

You have a life to live for yourself, but always remember, you are never too old to ask for help. A human can never perfect something in their life. You will always find someone better than you at a particular task, don't shy to ask for help, and never hold back to ask for any advice.

We feel low many a time in our lives. Sometimes we get some foul thoughts, but we shouldn't ever pounce on them. We should rather seek someone's company for comfort and sharing our concerns.

Conclusion

The ultimate success in life is the comfort you get at the end of every day. Life can never be fruitful, beneficial, and worth living for if we don't arrange our lives as resourceful human beings. Productive minds always find a way to counter things and make the best out of everything, and this is the art of living your life.

Chapter 2:

Why A few People Gets Most of the Rewards

The Amazon rainforest is one of the most diverse ecosystems on Earth. Scientists have cataloged approximately 16,000 different tree species in the Amazon. But despite this remarkable level of diversity, researchers have discovered that there are approximately 227 "hyper dominant" tree species that makeup nearly half of the rainforest. Just 1.4 percent of tree species account for 50 percent of the trees in the Amazon.

But why?

Imagine two plants growing side by side. Each day they will compete for sunlight and soil. If one plant can grow just a little bit faster than the other, it can stretch taller, catch more sunlight, and soak up more rain. The next day, this additional energy allows the plant to grow even more. This pattern continues until the stronger plant crowds the other out and takes the lion's share of sunlight, soil, and nutrients.

From this advantageous position, the winning plant can spread seeds and reproduce, which gives the species an even bigger footprint in the next generation. This process gets repeated repeatedly until the plants that are slightly better than the competition dominate the entire forest.

Scientists refer to this effect as an "accumulative advantage." What begins as a small advantage gets bigger over time. One plant only needs a slight edge, in the beginning, to crowd out the competition and take over the entire forest.

Winner-Take-All Effects

Something similar happens in our lives.

Like plants in the rainforest, humans are often competing for the same resources. Politicians compete for the same votes. Authors compete for the same spot at the top of the best-seller list. Athletes compete for the same gold medal. Companies compete for the same potential client. Television shows compete for the same hour of your attention.

The difference between these options can be razor-thin, but the winners enjoy massively outsized rewards.

The 1 Percent Rule

Small differences in performance can lead to unequal distributions when repeated over time. This is yet another reason why habits are so important. The people and organizations that can do the right things more consistently are more likely to maintain a slight edge and accumulate disproportionate rewards over time.

You only need to be slightly better than your competition, but if you can maintain a slight edge today and tomorrow and the day after that, then you can repeat the process of winning by just a little bit over and over again. And thanks to Winner-Take-All Effects, each win delivers outsized rewards.

We can call this The 1 Percent Rule. The 1 Percent Rule states that over time the majority of the rewards in a given field will accumulate to the people, teams, and organizations that maintain a 1 percent advantage over the alternatives. You don't need to be twice as good to get twice the results. You just need to be slightly better.

The 1 Percent Rule is not merely a reference to the fact that small differences accumulate into significant advantages but also the idea that those who are 1 percent better *rule* their respective fields and industries. Thus, the process of accumulative advantage is the hidden engine that drives the 80/20 Rule.

Chapter 3:

Why You're Demotivated By Lack of Clarity

Clarity is key to achieving any lasting happiness or success.

Demotivation is almost certain without clarity.

Always have a clear vision of what you want and why you want it.

Every detail should be crystal clear as if it were real.

Because it is.

Mustn't reality first be built on a solid foundation of imagination.

Your skills in visualisation and imagination must be strong to build that foundation.

You must build it in the mind and focus on it daily.

You must believe in it with all your heart and your head will follow.

Create it in the mind and let your body build it in reality.

That is the process of creation.

You cannot create anything in reality without clarity in the mind.

Even to make a cup of coffee, you must first imagine making a cup of coffee.

It doesn't take as much clarity as creating an international company,

but focus and clarity are required nonetheless.

The big goals often take years of consistent focus, clarity and commitment.

That is why so few succeed.

Demotivation is a symptom of lack of direction.

To have direction you must have clarity.

The Accomplished Woman

To have clarity you must have a clearly defined vision of you future.

Once you have this vision, never accept anything less.

Clarity and vision will begin your journey,

but your arrival depends on stubbornness and persistence.

Before you start you must decide to never quit, no matter what happens.

Clarity of your why will decide this for you.

Is the pain you are about to endure stronger than your reasons?

If you are currently demoralised by lack of clarity,

sit down and decide what will really make you happy.

Once you have decided, begin to make it feel real with pictures around your house.

Listen to motivational music and speeches daily to build your belief in you.

Visit where you dream you will be one day.

Get a feel for your desired new life.

Create actions that will build clarity in your vision.

Let it help you adjust to your new and future reality.

Slowly adjust your vision upwards.

Never adjust downwards.

Never settle for less.

The more real your vision feels the more likely it will be.

Begin to visualise living it.

Before long you will be living it.

Adopt the mannerisms of someone who would be in that position.

When you begin to believe you are important, others will follow.

Carry yourself like a champion.

Soon you will be one.

Have clarity you have about who you are.

Have clarity about what you are going to do.

Motivate yourself to success.

Once you step on that path you will not want to return to the you of yesterday.

You will be committed to becoming even better tomorrow.

You will be committed to being the new person you've always known you could be.

Always strive to get another step closer to your vision.

Work until that vision becomes clearer each day.

Have faith that each week more opportunities for progression will present themselves to you.

Clarity is the key to your success.

Chapter 4:

How To Improve Your

Communication Skills

Today we're going to talk about a topic that could help you be a better communicator with your spouse, your friends, and even your colleagues and bosses. Being able to express yourself fluently and eloquently is a skill that is incredibly important as it allows us to express our thoughts and ideas freely and fluently in ways that others might understand.

When we are able to communicate easily with others, we are able to build instant rapport with them and this allows us to appear better than we actually are. We may be able to cover some of our flaws if we are able to communicate our strengths better.

So how do we actually become better communicators? I believe that the easiest way to begin is to basically start talking with more people. It is my experience that after spending much time on my own without much social interaction, that i saw my standard of communication dropped quite drastically. You see, being able to talk well is essentially a social skill, and without regular practice and use, you just simply can't improve it. I saw that with irregular use of social interaction, the only skill that actually improved for me was texting. And we all know that texting is a very impersonal way to communicate and does not actually translate to real world fluency in person to person conversations.

Similarly, watching videos on communication and reading tips and tricks really does not help at all unless you apply it in the real world. And to have regular practice, you need to start by either inviting all your friends out to a meal so that you can strike up conversations and improve from there, or by maybe joining a social interaction group class of sorts that would allow you to practice verbal communication skills. If u were to ask me, I believe that making the effort to speak to your friends and colleagues is the best way to begin. And you can even ask them for feedback if there are any areas that they find you could improve on. Expect genuine feedback and criticisms as they go if you hope to improve, and do not take them personally.

It is with my personal experience that i became extremely rusty when it came to talking to friends at one point in my life, when i was sort of living in isolation. I find it hard to connect even with my best friend, and i found it hard to find topics to discuss about, mainly because i wasn't really living much to begin with, and there was nothing i was experiencing in life that was really worth sharing. If you stop living life, you stop having significant moments, you stop having problems that need solving, and you stop having friends that needs supporting. I believe the best way is to really try to engage the person you are talking to by asking them very thoughtful questions and by being genuinely interested in what they have to say. Which also coincidentally ties into my previous video about being a good listener. which you should definitely check out if you haven't done so already.

Being a good listener is also a big part of being a good communicator. The other part being able to respond in a very insightful way that isn't patronising. We can only truly connect with the person we are talking to if we are able to first understand on an empathetic level, what they are going through, and then to reply with the same level of compassion and empathy that they require of us.

With colleagues and bosses, we should be able to strike up conversations that are professional yet natural. And being natural in the way we communicate takes practice from all the other social interactions that precede us.

I believe that being a good communicator really takes time and regular practice in order for it to come one day and just click for us. For a start, just simply try to be friendly and place yourself out of your comfort zone, only then can you start to see improvements.

I challenge each and everyone of you today who are striving to be better communicators to start asking out your friends and colleagues for coffees and dinners. Get the ball rolling and just simply start talking. Over time, it will just come naturally to you. Trust me.

Chapter 5:

6 Ways To Attract Anything You Want In Life

It is common human nature that one wants whatever one desires in life. People work their ways to get what they need or want. This manifestation of wanting to attract things is almost in every person around us. A human should be determined to work towards his goal or dreams through sheer hard work and will. You have to work towards it step by step because no matter what we try or do, we will always have to work for it in the end. So, it is imperative to work towards your goal and accept the fact that you can't achieve it without patience and dedication.

We have to start by improving ourselves day by day. A slight change a day can help us make a more considerable change for the future. We should feel the need to make ourselves better in every aspect. If we stay the way we are, tomorrow, we will be scared of even a minor change. We feel scared to let go of our comfort zone and laziness. That way, either we or our body can adapt to the changes that make you better, that makes you attract better.

1. Start With Yourself First

We all know that every person is responsible for his own life. That is why people try to make everything revolves around them. It's no secret that everyone wants to associate with successful, healthy, and charming people. But, what about ourselves? We should also work on ourselves to become the person others would admire. That is the type of person people love. He can also easily attract positive things to himself. It becomes easier to be content with your desires. We need to get ourselves together and let go of all the things we wouldn't like others doing.

2. Have A Clear Idea of Your Wants

Keeping in mind our goal is an easy way to attract it. Keep reminding yourself of all the pending achievements and all the dreams. It helps you work towards it, and it enables you to attract whatever you want. Make sure that you are aware of your intentions and make them count in your lives. You should always make sure to have a crystal-clear idea of your mindset, so you will automatically work towards it. It's the most basic principle to start attracting things to you.

3. Satisfaction With Your Achievements

It is hard to stop wanting what you once desired with your heart, but you should always be satisfied with anything you are getting. This way, when you attract more, you become happier. So, it is one of the steps to draw things, be thankful. Be thankful for what you are getting and what you haven't. Every action has a reason for itself. It doesn't mean just to let it be. Work for your goals but also acknowledge the ones already achieved by you in life. That way you will always be happy and satisfied.

4. Remove Limitations and Obstacles

We often limit ourselves during work. We have to know that there is no limit to working for what you want when it comes to working for what you want. You remove the obstacles that are climbing their way to your path. It doesn't mean to overdo yourselves, but only to check your capability. That is how much pressure you can handle and how far you can go in one go. If you put your boundaries overwork, you will always do the same amount, thus, never improving further. Push yourself a little more each time you work for the things you want in life.

5. Make Your Actions Count

We all know that visualizing whatever you want makes it easier to get. But we still cannot ignore the fact that it will not reach us unless we do some hard work and action. Our actions speak louder than words, and they speak louder than our thoughts. So, we have to make sure that our actions are built of our brain image. That is the way you could attract the things you want in life. Action is an essential rule for attracting anything you want in life.

6. Be Optimistic About Yourselves

Positivity is an essential factor when it comes to working towards your goals or dreams. When you learn to be optimistic about almost everything, you will notice that everything will make you satisfied. You will attract positive things and people. Negative vibes will leave you disappointed in yourself and everyone around you. So, you will have to practice positivity. It may not be easy at first while everyone around you is pushing you to negativity. That is where your test begins, and you have to prove yourself to them and yourself. And before you know it, you are attracting things you want.

Conclusion

Everyone around us wants to attract what they desire, but you have to start with yourself first. You only have to focus on yourself to achieve what you want. And attracting things will come naturally to you. Make sure you work for your dreams and goals with all your dedication and determination. With these few elements, you will be attracting anything you want.

Chapter 6:

Block Out The Critics and Detractors

There is drama everywhere around us. In fact, our whole life is a drama. A drama that has more complex turns and thrillers than the best thriller ever to be made on a cinema screen.

This drama isn't always a result of our own actions. Sometimes we do something stupid to contribute towards anarchy. But mostly the things happening around us seem to be a drama because the critics make a hell out of everything.

We get sucked into things that and someone else's opinions because we do not know what we are doing.

It may sound cliche but remember that it doesn't matter what anyone else says. In fact, most discoveries and inventions got bad press when they were found or made. It was only after they are gone when people actually came to appreciate the true importance of those inventions.

The time will come sooner or later when you are finally appreciated for your work and your effort. But your work should not depend on what others will say.

Your work should not depend on the hope of appreciation or the fear of criticism, rather it should be done because it was meant to be done. You should put your heart and soul in it because you had a reason for all this and only you will reap the fruit, no matter what the world gets from it.

You don't need to do the best out there in the world and neither should you be judged on that standard. But you should put out the best YOU can do because that will someday shut out the critics as they start to see your true potential.

The work itself doesn't matter, but the effort you put behind it does. You don't need to be an insult to anyone who mocks you or criticizes you on even your best work. Empathy is your best approach to bullying.

You cannot possibly shut out every critic. You spend your whole life trying to answer to those meaningless least important people that weren't even able to make their own lives better. Because those who did make something of themselves didn't find it worthwhile to distract and degrade everyone else.

So you should try to spend your time more and more on your good work. Keep a straight sight without even thinking to look at one more ordinary critic who doesn't give a simple feeling of empathy towards your efforts.

You only need to put yourself in others' shoes and look at yourself through their eyes. If you can do that before them, you would have the best reply to any hurtful comment. And that my friend will be true silence.

People always come to gather around you when they see a cause they can relate to. So give them a cause. Give a ray of hope and motivation to people around you and you will finally get to get the critics on your side.

Your critics will help you get to the top from the hardest side there is.

Chapter 7:

When It Is Time To Let Go and Move On (Career)

Today we're going to talk about a topic that I hope will motivate you to quit that job that you hate or one that you feel that you have nothing more to give anymore.

For the purpose of this video, we will focus mainly on career as I believe many of you may feel as though you are stuck in your job but fear quitting because you are afraid you might not find a better one.

For today's topic, I want to draw attention to a close friend of mine who have had this dilemma for years and still hasn't decided to quit because he is afraid that he might not get hired by someone else.

In the beginning of my friend's career, he was full of excitement in his new job and wanted to do things perfectly. Things went pretty smoothly over the course of the first 2 years, learning new things, meeting new friends, and getting settled into his job that he thought he might stay on for a long time to come seeing that it was the degree that he had pursued in university. However when the 3rd year came along, he started to feel jaded with his job. Everyday he would meet ungrateful and sometimes mean customers who were incredibly self-entitled. They would be rude and he started dreading going to work more and more each day. This aspect of the job wore him down and he started to realise that he wasn't happy at all with his work.

Having had a passion for fitness for a while now, he realized that he felt very alive when he attended fitness classes and enjoyed working out and teaching others how to work out. He would fiddle with the idea of attending a teacher training course that would allow him to be a professional and certified fitness coach.

As his full time job started to become more of a burden, he became more serious about the prospect of switching careers and pursuing a new one entirely. At his job, realized that the company wasn't generous at all with the incentives and gruelling work hours, but he stayed on as he was afraid he wouldn't find another job in this bad economy. The fear was indeed real so he kept delaying trying to quit his job. Before he knew it 3 years more had passed and by this time he full on dreaded every single minute at his job.

It was not until he made that faithful decision one day to send in his resignation letter and to simultaneously pay for the teacher training course to become a fitness instructor did his fortunes start to change for him. The fortunes in this wasn't about money. It was about freedom. It was about growth. And it was about living.

We all know deep in our hearts when it is time to call it quits to something. When we know that there is nothing more that we can possibly give to our job. That no amount of time more could ever fulfill that void in us. That we just simply need to get out and do something different.

You see, life is about change. As we grow, our priorities change, our personalities change, our expectations change, and our passions and our interests change as well. If we stay in one place too long, especially in a field or in something that we have hit a wall at, we will feel stuck, and we will feel dread. We will feel that our time spent is not productive and we end up feeling hopeless and sorry for ourselves.

Instead when we choose to let go, when we choose to call time on something, we open up the doors for time on other ventures, and other adventures. And our world becomes brighter again.

I challenge each and everyone of you to take a leap of faith. You know deep in your hearts when it is time to move on from your current job and find the next thing. If you dont feel like you are growing, or if you feel that you absolutely hate your job because there is no ounce of joy that you can derive from it, move on immediately. Life is too short to be spending 10 hours of your life a day on something that you hate, that sucks the living soul out of you. Give yourself the time and space to explore, to find some other path for you to take. You will be surprised what might happen when you follow your heart.

I hope you learned something today, take care and I'll see you in the next one.

Chapter 8:

Why Are You Working So Hard

Your why,

your reason to get up in the morning,

the reason you act,

really is everything - for without it, there could be nothing.

Your why is the partner of your what,

that is what you want to achieve, your ultimate goal.

Your why will be what pushes you through the hard times on the path to your dreams.

It may be your children or a burning desire to help those less fortunate,

whatever the reason may be,

it is important to keep that in mind when faced with troubles or distractions.

Knowing what you want to do, and why you are doing it,

is of imperative importance for your life.

The tragedy is that most people are aiming for nothing.

They couldn't tell you why they are working in a certain field even if they tried.

Apart from the obvious financial payment,

They have no clue why they are there.

Is financial survival alone really a good motive to act?

Or would financial prosperity be guaranteed if you pursued greater personal preference?

Whatever your ambitions or preference in life,

make sure your why is important enough to you to guarantee your persistence.

Sometimes when pursuing a burning desire,

we can become distracted from the reason we are working.

Your why should be reflected in everything you do.

Once you convince yourself that your reason is important enough, you will not stop.

Despite the hardships, despite the fear, despite the loss and pain.

As long as you maintain a steady path of faith and resilience,

your work will soon start to pay off.

A light will protrude from the darkness and the illusionary troubles sent to test your faith will disappear as if they were never here.

Your why must be strong.

Your what must be as clear as the day is to you now.

And your faith must be eternal and unwavering.

Only then will the doors be opened to you.

This dream can be real, and will be.

When it is clear in the mind with faith, the world will move to show you the way.

The way will be revealed piece by piece, requiring you to take action and do the required work to bring your dream into reality.

Your why is so incredibly important.

The bigger your why, the greater the urgency, and the quicker your action will be.

Take the leap of faith.

Do what you didn't even know you could.

Never mind anyone else.

Taking the unknown path.

Perhaps against the advice of your family and friend,

But you know what your heart wants.

You know that even though the path will be dangerous, the reward will be tremendous.

The risks of not never finding out is too great.

The risk of never knowing if you could have done better is unfathomable.

You can always do better, and you must.

Knowing what is best for you may prove to be the most important thing for you.
How you feel about the work you are doing,
How you feel about the life you are living,
And how do you make the most of the time you have on this earth.
These may prove far more important than financial reward could ever do for you.

Aim to strike a balance.
A balance between working on what you are passionate about and building a wealthy financial life.
If your why and will are strong enough,
Success is all but guaranteed for you – no second guesses needed.

Aim for the sky,
However high you make it,
you will have proven you can indeed fly.

Chapter 9:

The Downside of Work-Life Balance

One way to think about work-life balance is with a concept known as The Four Burners Theory. Here's how it was first explained to me:

Imagine that a stove represents your life with four burners on it. Each burner symbolizes one major quadrant of your life.

1. The first burner represents your family.

2. The second burner is your friends.

3. The third burner is your health.

4. The fourth burner is your work.

The Four Burners Theory says that "to be successful, you have to cut off one of your burners. And to be successful, you have to cut off two."

The View of the Four Burners

My initial reaction to The Four Burners Theory was to search for a way to bypass it. "Can I succeed and keep all four burners running?" I wondered.

Perhaps I could combine two burners. "What if I lumped family and friends into one category?"

Maybe I could combine health and work. "I hear sitting all day is unhealthy. What if I got a standing desk?" Now, I know what you are thinking. Believing that you will be healthy because you bought a standing desk is like believing you are a rebel because you ignored the fasten seatbelt sign on an airplane, but whatever.

Soon I realized I was inventing these workarounds because I didn't want to face the real issue: life is filled with tradeoffs. If you want to excel in your work and your marriage, then your friends and your health may have to suffer. If you want to be healthy and succeed as a parent, then you might be forced to dial back your career ambitions. Of course, you are free to divide your time equally among all four burners, but you have to accept that you will never reach your full potential in any given area.

Essentially, we are forced to choose. Would you rather live a life that is unbalanced but high-performing in a certain area? Or would you rather live a life that is balanced but never maximizes your potential in a given quadrant?

Option 1: Outsource Burners

We outsource small aspects of our lives all the time. We buy fast food, so we don't have to cook. We go to the dry cleaners to save time on laundry. We visit the car repair shop, so we don't have to fix our automobile.

Outsourcing small portions of your life allow you to save time and spend it elsewhere. Can you apply the same idea to one quadrant of your life and free up time to focus on the other three burners?

Work is the best example. For many people, work is the hottest burner on the stove. It is where they spend the most time, and it is the last burner to get turned off. In theory, entrepreneurs and business owners can outsource the work burner. They do it by hiring employees.

The Four Burners Theory reveals a truth everyone must deal with: nobody likes being told they can't have it all, but everyone has constraints on their time and energy. Every choice has a cost.

Which burners have you cut off?

Chapter 10:

How To Focus on Creating Positive Actions

Only a positive person can lead a healthy life. Imagine waking up every day feeling like you are ready to face the day's challenges and you are filled with hope about life. That is something an optimist doesn't have to imagine because they already feel it every day. Also, scientifically, it is proven that optimistic people have a lower chance of dying because of a stress-caused disease. Although positive thinking will not magically vanish all your problems, it will make them seem more manageable and somewhat not a big deal.

Positive thinking is what leads to positive actions, actions that affect you and the people around you. When you think positively, your actions show how positive you are. You can create positive thinking by focusing on the good in life, even if it may feel tiny thing to feel happy about because when you once learn to be satisfied with minor things, you would think that you no longer feel the same amount of stress as before and now you would feel freer. This positive attitude will always find the good in everything, and life would seem much easier than before.

Being grateful for the things you have contributed a lot to your positive behavior. Gratitude has proven to reduce stress and improve self-esteem. Think of the things you are grateful for; for example, if someone gives you good advice, then be thankful to them, for if someone has helped you with something, then be grateful to them, by being grateful about minor things, you feel more optimistic about life, you feel that good things have always been coming to you. Studies show that making down a list of things you are grateful for during hard days helps you survive through the tough times.

A person laughing always looks like a happy person. Studies have shown that laughter lowers stress, anxiety, and depression. Open yourself up to humor, permit yourself to laugh even if forced because even a forced laugh can improve your mood. Laughter lightens the mood and makes problems seem more manageable. Your laughter is contagious, and it may even enhance the perspective of the people around us.

People with depression or anxiety are always their jailers; being harsh on themselves will only cause pain, negativity, and insecurity. So try to be soft with yourself, give yourself a positive talk regularly; it has proven to affect a person's actions. A positive word to yourself can influence your ability to regulate your feelings and thoughts. The positivity you carry in your brain is expressed through your actions, and who doesn't loves an optimistic person. Instead of blaming yourself, you can think differently, like "I will do better next time" or "I can fix this." Being optimistic about the complicated situation can lead your brain to find a solution to that problem.

When you wake up, it is good to do something positive in the morning, which mentally freshens you up. You can start the day by reading a positive quote about life and understand the meaning of that quote, and you may feel an overwhelming feeling after letting the meaning set. Everybody loves a good song, so start by listening to a piece of music that gives you positive vibes, that gives you hope, and motivation for the day. You can also share your positivity by being nice to someone or doing something nice for someone; you will find that you feel thrilled and positive by making someone else happy.

Surely you can't just start thinking positively in a night, but you can learn to approach things and people with a positive outlook with some practice.

PART 3

Chapter 1:

8 Tips to Become More Resilient

Resilience shows how well you can deal with the problems life throws at you and how you bounce back. It also means whether you maintain a positive outlook and cope with stress effectively or lose your cool. Although some people are naturally resilient, research shows that these behaviors can be learned. So, whether you are going through a tough time right now or you want to be prepared for the next step in your life, here are eight techniques you can focus on to become more resilient.

1. Find a Sense of Purpose

When you are going through a crisis or a tragedy, you must find a sense of purpose for yourself; this can play an important role in your recovery. This can mean getting involved in your community and participating in activities that are meaningful to you so every day you would have something to look forward to, and your mind wouldn't be focusing on the tragedy solely. You will be able to get through the day.

2. Believe in Your Abilities

When you have confidence in yourself that you can cope with the issues in your life, it will play an important role in resilience; once you become confident in your abilities, it will be easier for you to respond and deal with a crisis. Listen to the negative comments in your head, and once you do, you need to practice replacing them with positive comments like I'm good at my job, I can do this, I am a great friend/partner/parent.

3. Develop a Strong Social Network

It is very important to be surrounded by people you can talk to and confide in. When you have caring and supportive people around you during a crisis, they act as your protectors and make that time easier for you. When you are simply talking about your problems with a friend or a family member, it will, of course, not make your problem go away. Still, it allows you to share your feelings and get supportive feedback, and you might even be able to come up with possible solutions to your problems.

4. Embrace Change

An essential part of resilience is flexibility, and you can achieve that by learning how to be more adaptable. You'll be better equipped to respond to a life crisis when you know this. When a person is resilient, they use such events as opportunities to branch out in new directions. However, it is very likely for some individuals to get crushed by abrupt changes, but when it comes to resilient individuals, they adapt to changes and thrive.

5. Be Optimistic

It is difficult to stay optimistic when you are going through a dark period in your life, but an important part of resilience can maintain a hopeful outlook. What you are dealing with can be extremely difficult, but what will help you is maintaining a positive outlook about a brighter future. Now, positive thinking certainly does not mean that you ignore your problem to focus on the positive outcomes. This simply means understanding that setbacks don't always stay there and that you certainly have the skills and abilities to fight the challenges thrown at you.

6. Nurture Yourself

When you are under stress, it is easy not to take care of your needs. You can lose your appetite, ignore exercise, not get enough sleep. These are all very common reactions when you are stressed or are in a situation of crisis. That is why it is important to invest time in yourself, build yourself, and make time for activities you enjoy.

7. Develop Problem-Solving Skills

Research shows that when people are able to come up with solutions to a problem, it is easier for them to cope with problems compared to those who can not. So, whenever you encounter a new challenge, try making a list of potential ways you will be able to solve that problem. You can experiment with different strategies and eventually focus on developing a logical way to work through those problems. By practicing your problem-solving skills on a regular basis, you will be better prepared to cope when a serious challenge emerges.

8. Establish Goals

Crisis situations can be daunting, and they also seem insurmountable but resilient people can view these situations in a realistic way and set reasonable goals to deal with problems. So, when you are overwhelmed by a situation, take a step back and simply assess what is before you and then brainstorm possible solutions to that problem and then break them down into manageable steps.

Chapter 2:

How to Love Yourself First

It's so easy to tell someone "Love yourself" and much more difficult to describe *how* to do it. Learn and practice these six steps to gradually start loving yourself more every day:

Step 1: Be willing to feel pain and take responsibility for your feelings.

Step 1 is mindfully following your breath to become present in your body and embrace all of your feelings. It's about moving toward your feelings rather than running away from them with various forms of self-abandonment, such as staying focused in your head, judging yourself, turning to addictions to numb out, etc. All feelings are informational.

Step 2: Move into the intent to learn.

Commit to learning about your emotions, even the ones that may be causing you pain, so that you can move into taking loving action.

Step 3: Learn about your false beliefs.

Step 3 is a deep and compassionate process of exploration—learning about your beliefs and behavior and what is happening with a person or situation that may be causing your pain. Ask your feeling self, your inner child: "What am I thinking or doing that's causing the painful feelings of anxiety, depression, guilt, shame, jealousy, anger, loneliness, or emptiness?" Allow the answer to come from inside, from your intuition and feelings.

Once you understand what you're thinking or doing that's causing these feelings, ask your ego about the fears and false beliefs leading to the self-abandoning thoughts and actions.

Step 4: Start a dialogue with your higher self.

It's not as hard to connect with your higher guidance as you may think. The key is to be open to learning about loving yourself. The answers may come immediately or over time. They may come in words or images or dreams. When your heart is open to learning, the answers will come.

Step 5: Take loving action.

Sometimes people think of "loving myself" as a feeling to be conjured up. A good way to look at loving yourself is by emphasizing the action: "What can I *do* to love myself?" rather than "How can I *feel* love for myself?"

By this point, you've already opened up to your pain, moved into learning, started a dialogue with your feelings, and tapped into your spiritual guidance. Step 5 involves taking one of the loving actions you identified in Step 4. However small they may seem at first, over time, these actions add up.

Step 6: Evaluate your action and begin again as needed.

Once you take the loving action, check in to see if your pain, anger, and shame are getting healed. If not, you go back through the steps until you discover the truth and loving actions that bring you peace, joy, and a deep sense of intrinsic worth.

Over time, you will discover that loving yourself improves everything in your life—your relationships, health and well-being, ability to manifest your dreams, and self-esteem. Loving and connecting with yourself is the key to loving and connecting with others and creating loving relationships. Loving yourself is the key to creating a passionate, fulfilled, and joyful life.

Chapter 3:

Being Authentic

Today we're going to talk about the topic of authenticity. This topic is important because for many of us, we are told to put on a poker face and to act in ways that are politically correct. We are told by our parents, Teachers, and many other figures of authority to try to change who we are to fit society's norms and standards. Over time this constant act of being told to be different can end up forcing us to be someone who we are not entirely.

We start to behave in ways that are not true to ourselves. We start to act and say things that might start to appear rehearsed and fake, and we might not even notice this change until we hear whispers from colleagues or friends of friends that tell us we appear to be a little fake. On some level it isn't our fault as well, or it might be. Whatever the reason is, what we can do however is to make the effort to be more authentic.

So why do we need to be authentic? Well technically there's no one real reason that clearly defines why this is important. It actually depends on what we want to expect from others and in life in general. If we want to develop close bonds and friendships, it requires us to be honest and to be real. Our friends can tell very easily when it seems we are trying to hide something or if we are not being genuine or deceptive in the things we say. If people manage to detect that we are insincerity, they might easily choose to not be our friend or may start to distance themselves from us. If we are okay with that, then i guess being authentic is not a priority in this area.

When we choose to be authentic, we are telling the world that we are not afraid to speak our mind, that we are not afraid to be vocal of our opinions and not put on a mask to try and hide and filter how we present ourselves. Being authentic also helps people trust you more easily. When you are real with others, they tend to be real with you too. And this helps move the partnership along more quickly. Of course if this could also be a quick way to get into conflicts if one doesn't practice abit of caution in the things that they say that might be hurtful.

Being authentic builds your reputation as someone who is relatable. As humans we respond incredibly well to people who come across as genuine, kind, and always ready to help you in times of need. The more you open up to someone, they can connect with you on a much deeper emotional connection.

If you find yourself struggling with building lasting friendships, stop trying to be someone who you are not. You are not Kim Kardashian, Justin Bieber, or someone else. You are you, and you are beautiful. If there are areas of yourself you feel are lacking, work on it. But make sure you never try to hide the real you from others. You will find that life is much easier when you stop putting on a mask and just embracing and being you are meant to be all along.

I challenge each and everyone of you to consider adding authenticity into everything that you do. Let me know the changes that you have experienced as a result of that. I hope you learned something today, thank you so much for being there and I'll see you in the next one.

7 Ways To Get Clear On What You Want To Achieve In Life

Over time, you might be wondering what makes a person successful and why some people achieve success easier than others? The answer may differ from person to person, but it is a lot more than just setting a goal. As we become clear on our definition of success, it usually changes our perspective on life. With different insights such as these, our goal becomes more directive, and our achievement and motivation levels increase.

Here are 7 Ways To Get Clarity:

1. Success and Mindset Go Hand In Hand

The first and foremost tip of becoming successful is to know what success means for you. When you identify this, you will be directed towards your objective or goal, making it easier to achieve it. The second part is your mindset, as it plays a massive role in your success. You might notice that although you might be doing the same thing as hundreds of others, you still aren't getting anywhere. Therefore, you should develop a success mindset instead of being frustrated with it. Below are some ways to help you get clear on what you want to achieve in your life and develop a success mindset.

2. Be clear on your version of success:

Gaining clarity will positively affect your mindset, and it's vital to being and feeling successful. We might know what success means to us in our unconscious mind, but we aren't precisely implementing it in our everyday life. This can make it challenging to access our truth. The need to communicate with ourselves honestly and find some answers arises in such situations. We need to sit somewhere quiet, meditate, and ask ourselves about what we want in life. The answers might not come straight away, but it is essential to know your version of success and what you associate with it.

3. Stretch Yourself:

When setting our goals, it's crucial to step out of our comfort zone and include a few elements that will help us stretch and grow to achieve those goals. These might be doing something that you are usually not comfortable with or afraid of doing, such as public speaking, or simply learning a new skill that doesn't come easy on you. By doing this, you will help set a breakthrough goal that would represent a quantum leap. Examples of breakthrough goals include publishing a book, starting a business, or quitting your current job to get a new one. Of course, material goals are essential, but it all comes down to becoming a life master. The most significant benefit we receive while pursuing our dreams is who we become in the process. As motivational philosopher Jim Rohn advises, "You should set a goal big enough that in the process of achieving it, you become someone worth becoming."

4. Work on your goals daily:

Please make a list of all your goals and go through them every day to make sure your subconscious mind is focused on what you want. No matter how slow or small, your progress is, it counts as long as you decide not to give up and keep going. As the old joke runs, "How do you eat an elephant? One bite at a time." Similarly, steady progress in bite-sized chunks will eventually put the huge goals into reach. Thus, success isn't a one-time thing, but rather it is a system of gradual efforts.

5. Your goals should impact others:

There's not a single person on this earth who can say that he got successful on his own, without any help from anyone. The truth is, we always need a helping hand in the process of becoming something. As soon as we commit to big dreams and goals and go after them, our subconscious mind comes up with big creative ideas to make all of them happen. Then, we will start attracting the people, opportunities, and resources that we need to make our dreams come true. Big dreams not only inspire us but also compel others to play a bit too. When you discover that accomplishing something just isn't for you but also contributing to the betterment of others, it will accelerate the accomplishment of the goal.

6. Reflect and readjust without beating yourself up:

Reflection is one of the most critical success tips, yet it is one of the most crucial elements often ignored or forgotten to rush to the finishing line.

For each action that we take, we must be aware of whether it worked or not and then be prepared to change what we are doing until we achieve the outcome. Reflection helps us with all of this. It's ineffective if we just run full steam ahead blindly without pausing for a progress check. It is also important to be kind with yourself when reflecting, as beating yourself up will do no good to you. On the contrary, it will lower your self-esteem and makes it difficult for you to work up to your full potential.

7. Take good care of your mind and body:

Our mind and body play a vital role in how successful we become. Therefore, it is crucial to adopt the physiology and psychology of excellence. We must understand that our mind can impact our physical health and our body, too, has an enormous effect on our emotional state. If we feel low in energy and have negative thoughts, it can immensely effect how we perform our daily activities. Nurture your mind, body, and soul, your performance will excel, and you will experience more successful outcomes.

Conclusion:

Take a set of rules on what and how you want to achieve things in your life. Implement them daily and consistently, and you will begin to know what's important to you, which will give you a solid foundation to develop a clear mindset and achieve your goals.

Chapter 4:

The Daily Routine Experts for

Peak Productivity

What is the one thing we want to get done for a successful life? That is an effective daily routine to go through the day, every day. History is presented as an example that every high achiever has had a good routine for their day. Some simple changes in our life can change the outcome drastically. We have to take the experts' advice for a good lifestyle. We have to choose everything, from color to college, ourselves. But an expert's advice gives us confidence in our choice.

You have to set the bar high so that you get your product at the end of the day. Experts got their peak productivity by shaping their routine in such a way that it satisfies them. The productivity expert Tim Ferriss gave us a piece of simple yet effective advice for such an outcome. He taught us the importance of controlling oneself and how essential it is to provide yourself with a non-reactive practice. When you know how to control yourself, life gets more manageable, as it gives you the power to prevent many things. It reduces stress which gets your productivity out.

Another productive expert of ours, Cal Newport, gives us his share of information. He is always advising people to push themselves to their limits. He got successful by giving his deep work more priority than other work. He is managing multitasks at the same time while being a husband and a father. He is a true example of a good routine that leads to positive productivity. It would help if you decided what matters to you the most and need to focus on that. Get your priorities straight and work toward those goals. Construct your goals and have a clear idea of what your next step will be. It will result in increasing your confidence.

Now, the questions linger that how to start your day? Early is the answer. Early to bed and early to rising has been the motto of productive people. As Dan Ariely said, there is a must 3 hours in our day when our productivity is at its peak. A morning person hit more products, as it's said that sunrise is when you get active. Mostly from 8 o'clock to 10 o'clock. It's said that morning is the time when our minds work the sharpest. It provides you alertness and good memory ability. It is also called the "protected time." We get a new sense to think from, and then we get a sound vision of our steps and ideas to a routine of peak productivity.

Charles Duhigg is a known news reporter, works for the New York Times. He tells us to stop procrastinating and visualizing our next step in life. Not only does it give you confidence, but it also gives you a satisfactory feeling. You get an idea of the result, and you tend to do things more that way. This way, you get habitual of thinking about your next step beforehand. Habits are gradually formed. They are difficult to change but easy to assemble. A single practice can bring various elements from it. Those elements can help you learn the routine of an expert.

You will eventually fall into place. No one can change themselves in one day. Hard work is the key to any outcome. Productivity is the result of many factors but, an excellent daily routine is an integral part of it which we all need to follow. Once you fall into working constantly, you won't notice how productive you have become. It becomes a habit. There might be tough decisions along the way, which is typical for an average life. We need to focus on what's in front of us and start with giving attention to one single task on top of your priority list. That way, you can achieve more in less time. These are some factors and advice to start a daily routine for reaching the peak of productivity with the help of some great products.

Chapter 5:

What Every Successful Person Knows, but Never Says

Every person you meet will have a slightly different definition of what success is to them. Whether the goal is centered around finance, health, relationships, or their career, the point of "Success" is subjective. No matter what it looks like.. we all desire to achieve it in one way or another. We desire to achieve, excel, and gain; this is just a part of human nature.

When we decide to reach for success or set ourselves a new goal, it's obvious that at the point we are at, we have less understanding, knowledge, or skills than someone who has already reached that goal.

So it can be said that when we set a goal, we not only set a challenge to achieve something specific, we set ourselves a challenge to become the person who can achieve that thing. We do this through gaining new skills, practice and determination.

What Every Successful Person Knows but You Won't Hear Them Say

Often when we are at the starting point of attempting to achieve something new, a goal can feel overwhelming. We can feel as though the goal itself is HUGE or that perhaps we aren't capable of achieving it at all.

But the thing about success is that it's a process.

Malcolm Gladwell's book Outliers stated that it takes 10,000 hours of practice to become a master of something. This is a theory, of course, which will vary from person to person, but the point is clear. There is no such thing as overnight success. It takes years to become successful.

People generally don't talk about this part of becoming successful. Maybe because most of us don't want to hear the reality. In a world of instant gratification, perhaps the idea of long-term hard work is too difficult to swallow. The truth is, not only does it take years to become successful at something, but at the beginning of your journey, you're probably going to suck at it.

Yep. There will likely be a bunch of time, be it days, weeks, months, or years of you learning to be great at something that you simply won't be any good at. This is partly why many people never try new things. The idea of not being immediately brilliant at something is too much for their ego to bear.

It's kind of sad to think about how many people never try anything new or set themselves a goal because they feel like they need to be good straight away.

You Don't!

You can't! It's completely necessary not to be good at some stuff. How will you grow and evolve and get better at anything if you don't suck a little bit to start with?

How to Acknowledge The Unhappy Moments?

In today's video we will talk about how we can embrace the unhappiness moments in our lives and turn them into power and strength that will carry us through life gracefully.

We all have moments in life when we are not happy, we're scared, we're apprehensive, mildly depressed even, and the pain is difficult to endure. Whether it be because we have lost a friend, someone we love, or that we are simply not happy at our jobs. There could be a million reasons for our unhappiness.

In these trying times we only want an escape. To escape from our pain, our unhappy feelings because we are not ready to deal with the things that are going wrong in our lives. We don't want to acknowledge our unhappy moments because this makes us grieve and inflict more pain.

All these ways of avoiding the acknowledgment only perpetuate our feelings in long run. Avoidance only brings us misery and suffering in the long run. It keeps us from living to our fullest potential. It keeps us from the very fact that there is light at the end of the tunnel, and that we need to keep moving forward.

It is very important that you acknowledge your unhappy moments because you can only move forward with confidence once you accept that life being unhappy is simply a part of life. How can you admire happiness and the joys in your life if you have not gone through any unhappy moments? If you have nothing to compare it to?

It is not always easy to acknowledge the unhappy moments in life. But here are 5 powerful ways to help you along with the process.

Recognize the Reason of your unhappiness

First step of acknowledgment is to recognize the problem, find the real reason why you are unhappy. If, for example, you think you are not happy at your job, instead of pointing fingers at the obvious issues you are facing, ask yourself the deeper questions. Questions like, do I feel like I belong here? Do I feel I'm making a difference? Is what I am doing fulfilling my true desires? If the answer to those questions is a resounding no, it could be that your heart is, at that very moment, not in this job. You might be feeling as though you are spinning on a hamster wheel, going around in circles with nowhere in sight. It is very important to understand the true reason for your unhappiness because you cannot cut the stem and think that the tree will not grow again.

Take a moment and stop

Once you have found the problem, take a moment, and just stop right there. Don't suppress the feelings. Take a deep breath and sit with it for a while. Just sit there and be with it. Acknowledge that you have identified the essence of the unhappiness that had been festering in you for a while. And be glad that you now have something to work with to change your situation.

Accept what it is

Once you have found the root of the problem it's time to accept it. As Thick Nhat mentioned in his book "Peace is every step". He writes that it is important to mentally acknowledge our feelings. Say out loud if you feel like it, "I can accept that I am experiencing intense unhappiness right now. And that it is okay. And that I will be okay."

Once you have embraced your moments of unhappiness you can overcome the feelings and move forward with peace.

If you are embracing your moments of unhappiness, you can create a mental space and see around it instead of being enmeshed in them. This space will open new doors and help you overcome your feelings as you embrace new beginnings that will soon come your way.

Plan Next Best Move

Now that you have successfully identified the reason for your unhappiness, it is time to find out what your next best move is. In life we never really know what the next right move is, we can only hope and trust that our decisions will work for us in the end.

Take the time to write down the things you want and the things that can change your situation. Things that can potentially move you out from a place of unhappiness. Going back to the previous problem that we have discussed, if it is your job that is causing distress in your life, what are the potential ways you can apply to mitigate the problem, would it be to quit or could you find a compromise somewhere. Talking to a colleague, a friend, or even your boss to let you explore your areas of creativity and things you excel at could be a welcome change.

Whatever the potential may be, no matter how big or small, you have the power to change your situation. Don't stay trapped in that situation for too long as it will only bring you down further along the road.

Believe Things Will Work Out In The End

Hope is a very powerful thing. Now that we have a plan, we need to have faith and just believe that our actions will pay off. We can never predict the future, and so taking one step at a time is the best thing we can do. We have to believe that whatever we are doing to change our situation will turn our unhappiness around sooner or later.

Final Thoughts

Happy and unhappy moments are part of life, like day and night, light, and darkness.

If you only believe in one thing, believe that change is the only constant and that bad times don't last forever. You will be happy again and you will move forward gracefully. And this is only possible if acknowledge your unhappy moments.

Happiness Is just right around the corner.

Chapter 6:

Practicing Visualisation For Your Goals

Today we're going to talk about visualisation and why I think all of you should practice some form of visualisation everyday to help keep you on track to the future that you can see yourself living in maybe 5 or 10 years down the road.

So before we begin today's video, i want you to write down some of the goals that you want to achieve. These goals need not be entirely monetary, it could also be finding a partner, having a kid, having lots of friends, playing in a tournament of some elite sport, playing fluent guitar, skateboarding like a pro, or even working at the Apple store maybe... any personal goals and dreams that you might think u want.

And In terms of monetary goals, it could be the kind of income level and the kinds of material possessions that you wish you had, for example a dream car of yours, a pretty landed house or apartment in a prestigious neighbourhood, and nice flat screen Tv, a 10k diamond ring. Or whatever it may be. No matter how ridiculous, i want you to write these down.

Alright now that we have got this list in your hands, lets talk about what visualisation is and how it can be a powerful tool to help you actually achieve your goals.

What visualisation essentially is in a nutshell, is that it helps you step into the shoes of your future self, whether that may be 10 mins in the future, 10 years into the future, or even when you are at your death bed.

So why would we want to even think or imagine ourselves in the future when people have been telling us to be present and living in the moment etc. People including myself in my other videos. Well you see, the difference is that with visualisation, we are not looking into our past successes and failures as factors that influence our present state of mind, but rather to create a picture of a person that we want to be in the future that we can be proud of. A person that we think and aspire to become. Whether that be emulating an already rich or successful person, or simply just choosing to see yourself in possession of these things and people that you want in your life. Visualisation can help us mentally prepare ourselves for our future and help us solidify and affirm the actions that we need to take right now at this very moment to get to that end point.

Visualisation is such a powerful tool that when done correctly and consistency, our brain starts to blur the line between our present reality and our future self. And we are able to retrain and rewire our brain to function in the way that helps us achieve those goals by taking action more readily. If we have chosen to visualise ourselves as a pro tennis player, however far fetched it may seem, we have already decided on some level deep down that we are going to become that person no matter what it takes. And on a mental level, we have already committed to practicing the sport daily to achieve that outcome. If it is an income goal we hope to achieve, by visualising the person we hope to become who earns maybe $100k a month, yes it might sound far fetched again, but it is certainly not impossible, we will take actions that are drastically different than what we are doing today to make that goal happen. A person who visualises themselves making $100k a month will say and do things that are completely different from someone who tells themselves that they are okay to make just $2000 a month.

The action and effort taken is on a whole other level. A person who says they want to stay an amateur tennis player will do things differently than someone who visualises themselves becoming the top player of the sport who is ready to win grand slams.

With these two examples in mind, now i want you to take that list that we have created at the start of the video, and i want you to now place yourself inside of your imagination, I want you to start picturing a future you that has already been there done that. A future you who has got everything that he ever wanted, friends, family, money, career, sports, hobbies, travel, seeing the world, all of it. And I want you to visualise how you actually got to that point. What were the actions that you took to get there. How much time did you have to spend on each activity each day, day in and day out, and the level of commitment and desire that you needed to have, the belief that you will and have achieved your wildest dreams, how that must have felt, the emotion associated with reaching your goals, and becoming the person that you've always known you could be.

As this is your first time, i want you to spend at least 5-10mins trying to see yourself in your future shoes. It might not come right away as even visualisation takes practice. When we are so used to not using our imagination, it can be hard to reactivate that part of the brain. If you do not see it right now, i want you to keep going at it daily until that person in your head becomes clearer and clearer to you.

It might be easier to just see yourself as the next Warren Buffet, Jeff Bezos, Steve Jobs, Roger Federer, or whoever idol and superstar you wish to emulate. When you aim to emulate their success, you will mimic the actions that they take, and that could be a good way to start. Even a small change in your attitude and actions can go a long way.

Now that you have had a taste of the power of visualisation, I want you to practice visualisation on a daily basis. Again, everything boils down to consistency, and the more u practice seeing yourself as a successful person in life regularly, the more you believe that you can get there. Try your very best to pair that feeling with immense emotion. The feeling you get when you finally reached the summit. It will give you the best chance of success at actually following through with your goals and dreams.

To keep yourself motivated each day to practice visualisation, click on this link and save it to your favourites of daily habits. Refer to meditation series.

This has been quite an interesting topic to make for me as I have used visualisation myself with great success in helping me take consistent action, something that I struggle with daily, to reprogram my mind to work hard and stay the path.

Chapter 7:

How to Build Skills That Are

Valuable

The most valuable skills you can have in life and work are rarely taught in school, never show up on a resume, and are consistently overlooked and underappreciated. But there's some good news: It costs nothing to develop them, and you have the opportunity to do so.

Here's how

1. The Ability To Pay Attention

The shorter the average attention span gets, the more valuable your ability to focus becomes.

It's a huge competitive advantage to be able to pay attention to things for an extended period (and unfortunately, what passes for an extended period these days may be as little as 10 minutes).

The ability to pay attention helps you learn, communicate, be productive, and see opportunities others miss, among countless other things.

Two ways to improve your ability to pay attention:

- Practice single-tasking — read a book, watch a movie, or find some other thing to do for an extensive amount of time without allowing yourself to do anything else during that time. No side conversations. No checking your phone. Nothing but focus on that one thing.

- Become intentional with how you use your phone (and for the love of God, turn off your notifications!).

2. The Ability To Follow Directions

This one takes your improved ability to pay attention a step further.

Every aspect of your life and career involves directions —customers tell you what they want, your boss tells you what she needs to be done, and the people you care about tell you what they expect of you.

It's one thing to pay attention to instructions, but it's another to accurately follow them.

The best qualifications in the world won't land you a job if your application doesn't include the employer's requested details.

Your company won't care about your innovative ideas if they don't align with the problems they asked you to solve.

And the reason Facebook Ads may not work for you isn't that Facebook ads don't work — it's because you don't know the right ways to use them. The ability to follow directions serves as a filter that keeps otherwise qualified people from succeeding — and most of them don't even realize their struggles are rooted in this weakness.

Don't let that be you.

Two ways to improve your ability to follow directions:

1. Ask for directions on how to do things more often. Practice makes perfect.

2. Give directions to other people. Take something you know how to do (like write a blog post, for example), and write up directions to help others do it the way you do (like I did here). Teaching is a great way to learn, and the process of creating directions will help you recognize the importance of little steps in directions you get from others.

The point of this post isn't to make you feel overwhelmed. The truth is, you already have these skills — we all do. But I wrote this because I've noticed many people don't think about these abilities as skills and therefore don't do much to hone them.

Chapter 8:

Overcoming Fear and Self-Doubt

The lack of belief most people have is the reason for their failure at even the smallest things in life. The biggest killer of dreams is the lack of belief in ourselves and the doubt of failure.

We all make mistakes. We all have some ghosts of the past that haunt us. We all have something to hide. We all have something that we regret. But what you are today is not the result of your mistakes.

You are here because of your struggles to make those things go away. You are here now with the power and strength to shape your present and your future.

Our mind is designed to take the shape of what we hold long enough inside it. The things we frequently think about ultimately start filling in the spaces within our memory, so we have to be careful. We have to decide whether we want to stay happy or to hold on to the fear we once wanted to get rid of.

The human spirit and human soul are colored by the impressions we ourselves decide to impose.

The reason why we don't want to explore the possibility of what to do is that subconsciously we don't believe that it can happen for us. We don't believe that we deserve it or if it was meant for us.

So here is something I suggest. Ask yourself, how much time in a day do you spend thinking about your dream? How much time do you spend working on your dreams everyday? What books did you read this year? What new skills have you acquired recently? What have you done that makes you worthy of your dream? Nothing?

Then you are on point with your doubt because you don't have anything to show for when the opportunity presents itself.

You don't succeed because you have this latent fear. Fear that makes you think about the consequences of what will happen if you fail even with all the good things on your hand?

I know that feeling but failure is there to teach you one important and maybe the most essential skill life can teach us; Resilience.

You rediscover your life once you have the strength to fight your every fear and every doubt because you have better things on your hand to care for.

You have another dream to pursue. Another horizon awaits you. Another peak to summit. It doesn't matter if you literally have to run to stand still. You got to do what you got to do, no matter the consequences and the sacrifices.

But failing to do what is required of you has no justifiable defense. Not even fear. Because your fears are self-imposed and you already have many wrong things going on for you right now.

Don't let fear be one of them. Because fear is the most subtle and destructive disease So inhale all your positive energies and exhale all your doubts because you certainly are a better person without them.

Structure Your Day With Tasks You Excel At and Enjoy

Today's video will probably appeal to people who have a say in the way they can structure their day. People who are working on their own businesses, or are freelancers. But it could also apply to those with full time jobs if your jobs allow flexibility.

For those who have been doing their own thing for a while, we know that it is not easy to put together a day that is truly enjoyable. We forget about doing the things we like and excel at, and start getting lost in a sea of work that we have to drag ourselves through doing.

If we don't have a choice, then I guess we can't really do anything about it. But if we do, we need to start identifying the tasks that require the most attention but the least effort on our part to do. Tasks that seem just about second-nature to us. Tasks that we would do even if nobody wanted to pay us. Tasks that allow our creativity to grow and expand, tasks that challenge us but not drain us, tasks that enriches us, or tasks that we simply enjoy doing.

The founding father of modern Singapore, one of the wealthiest countries in the world, Mr Lee Kuan Yew once said, find what works and just keep doing it over and over again. I would apply that to this situation as well. We have to find what works for us and just double down on it. The other stuff that we aren't good at, either hire someone else to do it, or find a way to do less of it or learn how to be good at it fast. Make it a challenge for ourselves. Who knows maybe you might find them enjoyable once you get a hang of it as well.

But for those things that already come naturally to us, do more of it. Pack a lot of time into at the start of the day. Dedicated a few hours of your day to those meaningful tasks that you excel at. You will find that once you get the creative juices and the momentum going, you will be able to conquer the other less pleasing tasks more easily knowing that you've already accomplished your goals for the day.

Start right now. Identify what those tasks that you absolutely love to do right now, work-wise, or whatever it may be, and just double down on it. Watch your day transform.

Chapter 9:

8 Steps To Develop Beliefs That Will Drive you To Success

'Success' is a broad term. There is no universal definition of success, it varies from person to person considering their overall circumstances. We can all more or less agree that confidence plays a key role in it, and confidence comes from belief.

Even our most minute decisions and choices in life are a result of believing in some specific outcome that we have not observed yet.

However, merely believing in an ultimate success will not bring fortune knocking at your door. But, it certainly can get you started—take tiny steps that might lead you towards your goal. Now, since we agree that having faith can move you towards success, let's look at some ways to rewire your brain into adopting productive beliefs.

Here are 8 Steps to Develop Beliefs That Will Drive You To Success:

1. Come Up With A Goal

Before you start, you need to decide what you want to achieve first. Keep in mind that you don't have to come up with something very specific right away because your expectations and decisions might change over time. Just outline a crude sense of what 'Achievement' and 'Success' mean to you in the present moment.

Begin here. Begin now. Work towards getting there.

2. Put Your Imagination Into Top Gear

"Logic will take you from A to B. Imagination will take you everywhere", said Albert Einstein.

Imagination is really important in any scenario whatsoever. It is what makes us humans different from animals. It is what gives us a reason to move forward—it gives us hope. And from that hope, we develop the will to do things we have never done before.

After going through the first step of determining your goal, you must now imagine yourself being successful in the near future. You have to literally picture yourself in the future, enjoying your essence of fulfilment as vividly as you can. This way, your ultimate success will appear a lot closer and realistic.

3. Write Notes To Yourself

Writing down your thoughts on paper is an effective way to get those thoughts stuck in your head for a long time. This is why children are encouraged to write down what is written in the books instead of memorizing them just by reading. You have to write short, simple, motivating notes to yourself that will encourage you to take actions towards your success. It doesn't matter whether you write in a notebook, or on your phone or wherever—just write it. On top of that, occasionally read what you've written and thus, you will remain charged with motivation at all times.

4. Make Reading A Habit

There are countless books written by successful people just so that they can share the struggle and experience behind their greatest achievements. In such an abundance of manuscripts, you may easily find books that portray narratives similar to your life and circumstances. Get reading and expand your knowledge. You'll get never-thought-before ideas that will guide you through your path to success. Reading such books will tremendously strengthen your faith in yourself, and in your success. Read what other successful people believed in—what drove them. You might even find newer beliefs to hold on to. No wonder why books are called 'Man's best friend'.

5. Talk To People Who Motivates You

Before taking this step, you have to be very careful about who you talk to. Basically, you have to speak out your goals and ambitions in life to someone who will be extremely supportive of you. Just talk to them about what you want, share your beliefs and they will motivate you from time to time towards success. They will act as powerful reminders.

Being social beings, no human can ever reject the gist of motivation coming from another human being—especially when that is someone whom you can rely on comfortably. Humans have been the sole supporter of each other since eternity.

6. Make A Mantra

Self-affirming one-liners like 'I can do it', 'Nothing can stop me', 'Success is mine' etc. will establish a sense of firm confidence in your subconscious mind. Experts have been speculative about the power of our subconscious mind for long. The extent of what it can do is still beyond our grasp. But nonetheless, reciting subtle mantras isn't a difficult task. Do it a couple of times every day and it will remain in your mind for ages, without you giving any conscious thought to it. Such subconscious affirmations may light you up in the right moment and show you the path to success when you least expect it.

7. Reward Yourself From Time To Time

Sometimes, your goals might be too far-fetched and as a result, you'll find it harder to believe in something so improbable right now. In a situation like this, what you can do is make short term objectives that ultimately lead to your main goal and for each of those objectives achieved, treat yourself with a reward of any sort—absolutely anything that pleases you. This way, your far cry success will become more apparent to you in the present time. Instant rewards like these will also keep you motivated and make you long for more. This will drive you to believe that you are getting there, you are getting closer and closer to success.

8. Having Faith In Yourself

Your faith is in your hands alone. How strongly you believe in what you deserve will motivate you. It will steer the way for self-confidence to fulfill your inner self. You may be extremely good at something but due to the lack of faith in your own capabilities, you never attempted it—how will you ever know that you were good at that? Your faith in yourself and your destined success will materialize before you through these rewards that you reserve for yourself. You absolutely deserve this!

Final Thoughts

That self-confidence and belief and yourself, in your capabilities and strengths will make you work towards your goal. Keep in mind that whatever you believe in is what you live for. At the end of the day, each of us believed in something that made us thrive, made us work and move forward. Some believed in the military, some believed in maths, some believed in thievery—everyone had a belief which gave them a purpose—the purpose of materializing their belief in this world. How strongly you hold onto your belief will decide how successful you will become

Chapter 10:

8 Ways To Love Yourself First

"Your task is not to seek for love, but merely to seek and find all the barriers within yourself that you have built against it." - Rumi.

Most of us are so busy waiting for someone to come into our lives and love us that we have forgotten about the one person we need to love the most – ourselves. Most psychologists agree that being loved and being able to love is crucial to our happiness. As quoted by Sigmund Freud, "love and work … work and love. That's all there is." It is the mere relationship of us with ourselves that sets the foundation for all other relationships and reveals if we will have a healthy relationship or a toxic one.

Here are some tips on loving yourself first before searching for any kind of love in your life.

1. Know That Self-Love Is Beautiful

Don't ever consider self-love as being narcissistic or selfish, and these are two completely different things. Self-love is rather having positive regard for our wellbeing and happiness. When we adopt self-love, we see higher levels of self-esteem within ourselves, are less critical and harsh with ourselves while making mistakes, and can celebrate our positive qualities and accept all our negative ones.

2. Always be kind to yourself:

We are humans, and humans are tended to get subjected to hurts, shortcomings, and emotional pain. Even if our family, friends, or even our partners may berate us about our inadequacies, we must learn to accept ourselves with all our imperfections and flaws. We look for acceptance from others and be harsh on ourselves if they tend to be cruel or heartless with us. We should always focus on our many positive qualities, strengths, and abilities, and admirable traits; rather than harsh judgments, comparisons, and self-hatred get to us. Always be gentle with yourself.

3. Be the love you feel within yourself:

You may experience both self-love and self-hatred over time. But it would be best if you always tried to focus on self-love more. Try loving yourself and having positive affirmations. Do a love-kindness meditation or spiritual practices to nourish your soul, and it will help you feel love and compassion toward yourself. Try to be in that place of love throughout your day and infuse this love with whatever interaction you have with others.

4. Give yourself a break:

We don't constantly live in a good phase. No one is perfect, including ourselves. It's okay to not be at the top of your game every day, or be happy all the time, or love yourself always, or live without pain. Excuse your bad days and embrace all your imperfections and mistakes. Accept your negative emotions but don't let them overwhelm you. Don't set high standards for yourself, both emotionally and mentally. Don't judge yourself for whatever you feel, and always embrace your emotions wholeheartedly.

5. Embrace yourself:

Are you content to sit all alone because the feelings of anxiety, fear, guilt, or judgment will overwhelm you? Then you have to practice being comfortable in your skin. Go within and seek solace in yourself, practice moments of alone time and observe how you treat yourself. Allow yourself to be mindful of your beliefs, feelings, and thoughts, and embrace solitude. The process of loving yourself starts with understanding your true nature.

6. Be grateful:

Rhonda Bryne, the author of The Magic, advises, "When you are grateful for the things you have, no matter how small they may be, you will see those things instantly increase." Look around you and see all the things that you are blessed to have. Practice gratitude daily and be thankful for all the things, no matter how good or bad they are. You will immediately start loving yourself once you realize how much you have to be grateful for.

7. Be helpful to those around you:

You open the door for divine love the moment you decide to be kind and compassionate toward others. "I slept and dreamt that life was a joy. I awoke and saw that life was service. I acted, and behold, and service was a joy." - Rabindranath Tagore. The love and positive vibes that you wish upon others and send out to others will always find a way back to you. Your soul tends to rejoice when you are kind, considerate, and compassionate. You have achieved the highest form of self-love when you decide to serve others. By helping others, you will realize that you don't need someone else to feel complete; you are complete. It will help you feel more love and fulfillment in your life.

8. Do things you enjoy doing:

If you find yourself stuck in a monotonous loop, try to get some time out for yourself and do the things that you love. There must be a lot of hobbies and passions that you might have put a brake on. Dust them off and start doing them again. Whether it's playing any sport, learning a new skill, reading a new book, writing in on your journal, or simply cooking or baking for yourself, start doing it again. We shouldn't compromise on the things that make us feel alive. Doing the things we enjoy always makes us feel better about ourselves and boost our confidence.

Conclusion:

Loving yourself is nothing short of a challenge. It is crucial for your emotional health and ability to reach your best potential. But the good news is, we all have it within us to believe in ourselves and live the best life we possibly can. Find what you are passionate about, appreciate yourself, and be grateful for what's in your life. Accept yourself as it is.

CPSIA information can be obtained
at www.ICGtesting.com
Printed in the USA
BVHW070314301121
622779BV00009B/604